# On the Road to Reading

## 101 Creative Activities for Beginning Readers

by Beatrice G. Davis, M.S., P.D.
illustrated by
Sheila Wigglesworth

For information regarding permission write to:

**Berrent Publications, Inc.**
1025 Northern Blvd.
Roslyn, NY 11576

On The Road To Reading

I.S.B.N.# 1-55743-225-2
B.P.I.# 19200
N.Y.C.# 55743-225-1

Printed in the United States.

# Table of Contents

# *Introduction*

Literacy learning is learning about language: spoken and written language. From the moment they are born, children are exposed to spoken language. As they listen and make sounds, children begin to understand and develop their own spoken language. Almost from this same moment, children are exposed to written language. As they look and, eventually, as they play, children begin to understand and develop reading and writing skills. Parents talk to their children and cherish their children's beginning sounds and early words.

Children are likely to have toys, clothes, and room decorations with their names on them or with letters of the alphabet incorporated into the design. Adults, as well as children, frequently wear clothes that have letters, words, or sayings on them. In addition, children see print in their environment every time they visit a supermarket, go for a drive, have a book read to them, walk down a street, go through a mall, watch TV, or see the mail that is delivered to their homes. All of these give children the message that those funny-looking things called letters and words are somehow used to communicate meaning.

Young children are creative and imaginative. Their worlds should be filled with varied opportunities for discovering, experimenting, exploring, and thinking. Children are usually interested in words. They like saying new words and grasping their different shades of meaning. Occasionally they invent words. Their play is a way of learning and finding out about their world.

Children learn best when they have the freedom to discover ideas and concepts for themselves. The activities in this book will help them learn to think, evaluate, and make decisions. When children have a reason for putting thoughts into words, and for asking and answering questions, they gain self-confidence and a sense of self-worth. These are probably the most important factors in achieving success in school and in life.

The purpose of this book is to help prepare children for literacy learning. Actual reading ability depends on each child's "inner clock"--that individual combination of emotional, neurological, and intellectual factors which make each child ready to read at a given time.

No matter when formal reading instruction begins in your children's school, you as a parent can and should take responsibility for helping them get a good start by building a foundation for literacy learning at home. Remember that parents are the first educators of their children. Children learn how to read when they go to school--parents can teach them to want to read by the example they set at home.

The following checklist outlines some of the experiences, background, and abilities that will help your child be ready for reading. Remember, all children are different. Additionally, they are ready to learn to read at different times. Don't push, but rather, be supportive.

 Throughout the book, this "auto" icon will appear to the left of any activity which you and your child can do in the car.

# School Readiness Checklist

**A checklist for beginning readers**

The child knows:

____ whole name ____ address ____ telephone
____ her/his date of birth ____ own age
____ names of any brothers and sisters
____ her/his parents' or caretakers' names
____

The child can:

____ recognize and say the names of colors
____ recognize and say the names of shapes
____ count to five using objects
____ say the letters of the alphabet

The child knows the difference between:

____ up and down ____ in and out
____ over and under ____ left and right
____ before and after ____ big and little
____ larger and smaller ____ hot and cold

Some school readiness behaviors:

____ listen to stories ____ have favorite stories read
____ make up rhymes ____ remember rhymes or lyrics
____ tell a story by looking at pictures
____ speak in sentences
____ participate in discussions
____ play with numbers
____ follow directions that have more than 1 step

Remember: Children should be able to do many, not all, of these by the time they reach kindergarten. Don't panic. These will all come in time.

Chapter

1

Developing
Whole
Language by
Reading
Together

# Developing Whole Language by Reading Together

*Whole language instruction is based on the theory that learning to read is a natural process of speaking, listening, and writing. Literacy learning is helped by many different experiences with language. The more varied language experiences children have, the better chance they have of becoming successful readers.*

*One of the easiest ways to prepare your children for reading success in school is to read with them at home. Reading to your children will help to expand their concepts of the world and the language we use to communicate in and about it. Read with your children regularly because it is a positive way to increase whole language development skills.*

# Part One
## DO's and DON'T's for Reading Aloud

### 1. Do...

Have your child sit on your lap as you read. This is another way of telling her/him that reading is a pleasurable activity.

### 2. Do...

Read rhymes such as Mother Goose, nonsense poems, fairy tales, fantasies, and folk tales, as well as contemporary stories.

## 3. Do...

Start with bright colored picture and story books that have characters close to your child's age. Other good books to start with are fanciful stories about animals that have human characteristics (talk to their children, live in a house, go to school) and stories that contain a lot of repetition.

## 4. Do...

Allow your child to choose the book or story she/he wants to hear even if it's one you've read many times before. Children like the comfort of hearing familiar language and story situations. Research has shown that repeated readings of a story improve a child's ability to interact with print.

**5. Do...**

Hold the book so your child can see that you always start reading from the front of the book; that you always read from the top to bottom and left to right; that the pages follow a specific order; and that you handle books with care.

**6. Do...**

Hold the book so that your child can see the page you are reading and so she/he can follow along.

**7. Don't...**

Reading to your child should not be stopped when she/he is able to read independently.

**8. Don't...**

Reading should not be started if you won't have enough time for both of you to enjoy the experience.

**9. Don't...**

Read-aloud time should not be treated as a chore to be gotten through as quickly as possible. You'll find that it can become a most pleasurable time that both you and your child will look forward to each day.

## 10. Do...

Show your child that reading is important to you. Let your child see you read for:

- *information*: newspapers, magazines

- *instruction*: recipes, knitting, sewing, "how to" books, model-making

- *pleasure*: React to what you're reading. Smile, laugh out loud, or just say something about what you've read.

## 11. Do...

Remember that children learn by imitation. When they see you reading and enjoying it, they'll want to do the same.

# Part Two
## Reading Activities

### 12. Family Read-Aloud Time

Establish a regular time for reading to and with your child. Try to incorporate it into your daily schedule. Even very young babies respond to the rhythm of story language long before they understand the meaning of the words. They respond to pictures, too. So take time to point out and talk about pictures as you read together.

### 13. Making Book Connections

Wherever possible, try to relate the events and characters in the story you are reading to people and situations in your child's life. This will help create a deeper understanding of the story.

### 14. Develop The Library Habit

Plan regular trips to the library. Prepare for one of your first visits by explaining how books are borrowed and returned. Allow enough time for browsing through the books. Try to limit the number of books your child checks out to two or three books. Check out a book or two for yourself. If your library has regularly scheduled story hours, try to attend. Make library day a special part of your family routine.

## 15. Ask Questions About The Book

Asking questions after your child reads is a wonderful way to help your child think about what she/he has read. Ask thinking questions but don't ask too many questions. Remember to have fun. Here are some questions you may want to ask:

Which part of the book did you like best/least?

Which part was the funniest? Nicest? Saddest? Happiest? Scariest?

Which part would you like to have happen to you?

Which words or scenes did you like?

Why do you think the (boy, girl, animal, man, woman) behaved that way?

What do you think will happen in the next book?

How would you have changed the way the story ended?

What would happen if...?

### 16. Magazine Subscriptions

If you can, give your child a subscription to a magazine written especially for children. <u>Ranger Rick</u> and <u>Big Backyard</u>, published by the National Wildlife Society and <u>World</u>, published by the National Geographic Society are particularly good for young children. Subscriptions make a wonderful gift because the gift arrives every month. It also shows children how print is used to communicate through the mail.

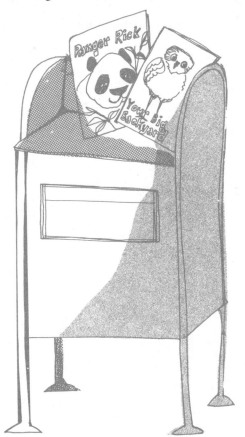

## 17. "Read" Wordless Picture Books

These are excellent for learning about story sequence (the order in which a story happens). The stories you create together will be uniquely yours. They can be varied each time you read them.

## 18. Talk About Books

As soon as your child is able to express her/himself verbally, be sure to take time to talk about a book or story after you have read it. Talking helps to clarify thoughts about a story

# Sorting and Classifying Activities

*Knowing that different things can be organized into specific groups will help your child to conceptualize and understand the relationships among things.*

### 19. Classification Lists

Talk about and make lists of things that belong together such as foods, toys, household items, and vehicles. As your child matures, the lists can be revised and refined. For example, you could have a list of sweet foods, spicy foods, fruits, vegetables, things that are found in a bedroom, things that are found in the kitchen, or different kinds of vehicles.

## 20. More Classification

"What kinds of games and activities can we play indoors? Outdoors? On rainy days? In the summertime? In the wintertime?"

## 21. Sorting Shapes

*Materials:*

construction paper or
       brown kraft paper
assorted blocks
felt or fabrics which are easily cut
scissors

*Directions:*

Cut paper and/or fabric into shapes which child can identify--circles, triangles, squares, and rectangles. Mix all shapes together. Your child must sort them according to shape. If you have blocks of similar shapes, be sure to include them so she/he can see that no matter what the material, the shape or form remains the same.

## 22. Sorting Colors

*Materials:*
assorted beads
crayons
felt tip pens
colored construction paper
any of the materials used for sorting
shapes


*Directions:*
Present the child with a variety of
the materials.  Items must then be
grouped by colors. (All reds together,
all blues, all greens...)

Remember, at first, use only as many colors as you know your child can comfortably identify. You can add new ones as the child learns to differentiate between such colors as aqua and blue, fuchsia and purple.

*Variation:*

*Combine sorting shapes with sorting colors. For example: Make a pile of green triangles, brown circles, orange squares...*

## 23. Sorting Household Items

Let your child help you when you sort and store household items such as groceries, silverware, clothing, games, and tools. Talk about your reasons for grouping some things by shape, some things by size, some things by color, and some things by purpose or function.

## 24. Seeing Relationships I

*Materials:*

Pictures of clothing, toys, foods, and flowers that are cut from magazines, old books, and catalogs

*Directions:*

Give your child five or six pictures of different things that must be placed in groups that go together.

## 25. Seeing Relationships II

### Materials:

Pairs of things that usually go together such as a bowl and spoon, paper and pencil, jacks and ball, paint brush and paint

### Directions:

Randomly place several pairs of objects, such as those listed above, on a table or the floor. Ask your child to match up the things that go together. Encourage her or him to talk about the reasons for pairing the objects in a specific way.

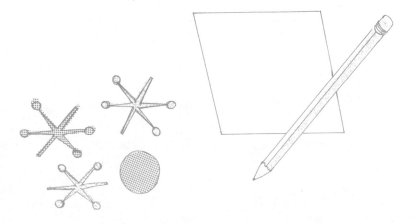

## 26. Seeing Relationships III

### Materials:

Prepare pictures of several things that go together in a house, in the kitchen, or at the playground. Add one or two pictures of things that don't fit the category.

### Directions:

Ask your child to find the pictures that don't belong. Ask her/him to tell why they don't belong.

*Variation:*

> *Group small toys or objects that go together by color, function, or shape. Add one or two things that don't fit the category. The child must discover the different object and tell why it doesn't belong. Example: A red block, a red bead, a red pencil, and a blue button. (The button is not the same color.)*

# Vocabulary Development

*Increasing the scope of your child's understanding of concepts and the vocabulary related to them is probably one of the single most important ways you can help prepare her/him for reading instruction. Many of the everyday activities that take place in your home are ideal for developing and enhancing vocabulary. By using a varied vocabulary and encouraging your child to do the same you will be making a major contribution to his or her readiness for literacy learning.*

## 27. Cooking

Let your child help with easy cooking activities. Use words such as whipping, stirring, beating, broiling, frying, freezing, chilling, setting, blending, and measuring. In addition, be sure to identify the utensils you use such as ladle, spatula, tablespoon, teaspoon, and tongs.

## 28. Household Chores

There are many words associated with doing chores both in and out of the house. Children love to help with chores. Words such as vacuum, broom, laundry, rake, mop, dust-cloth, wax, cleanser, soil, and hose will soon become part of your children's vocabulary if they have experiences with them.

## 29. TV Words

There are many words that are specifically used when we talk about television. Why not use them when you discuss TV with your child? Words such as program, schedule, broadcast, rerun, special, comedy, drama, newscaster, and reporter can all be used to enlarge your child's vocabulary.

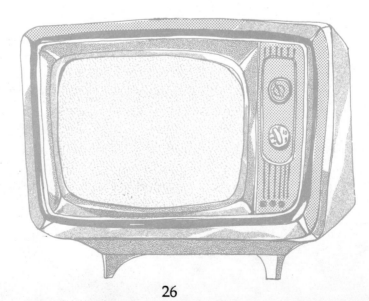

26

## 30. Neighborhood Excursions

Each time you walk or drive through your neighborhood you have an opportunity to increase your child's vocabulary. Places such as the post office, neighborhood shops, supermarkets, railroad stations, beauty salons, and schools--each have special vocabulary associated with them. Be sure to talk about the places you pass as well as about the places you are going to visit.

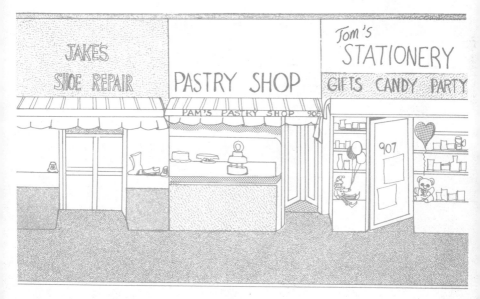

## 31. Weather Words

Make a list of all the weather words your child knows. Keep a chart recording the weather for several days or weeks. Use symbols such as pictures of the sun, an umbrella, or a snowman to show what the weather is like each day. Let your child draw a picture (or cut out pictures and paste them on the chart) to show the kind of clothes she or he wears on a sunny day, a rainy day, a snowy day, a windy day, a hot day, or a cold day.

| SUNDAY | MONDAY | TUESDAY | WEDNESDAY | THURSDAY | FRIDAY | SATURDAY |
|--------|--------|---------|-----------|----------|--------|----------|
| 1 | 2 | 3 | 4 | 5 | 6 | 7 |
| 8 | 9 | 10 | 11 | 12 | 13 | 14 |
| 15 | 16 | 17 | 18 | 19 | 20 | 21 |
| 22 | 23 | 24 | 25 | 26 | 27 | 28 |
| 29 | 30 | 31 | | | | |

## 32. Sports Activity Words

How many words do you know that tell about baseball? Football? Swimming? Soccer? Tag? Bowling? Bicycle riding?

## 33. Words that Tell About...

Talk about and make lists of words that tell about people, toys, clothing, cars, games, families, foods, fruits, vegetables, or any other categories which are of interest to you and your child. Each list should have the same kind of title. For example: *Words That Tell About People, Words That Tell About Food*. Add to the lists as new words are learned. You can combine the lists into a booklet which your child can illustrate. It can then be used as a beginning dictionary. Making these lists is also a good way to develop classification skills.

Words That Tell About Toys

choo-choo train

doll

teddy bear

ball

Words That Tell About Food

cereal

popcorn

bread

milk

juice

## 34. Stranger In The Family

Once children are aware of groups of words that are related (because they are about the same kinds of things), they can play *Stranger In The Family*.

### Directions:

Say: *triangle, square, purple, circle.* Child must guess which word is the "stranger." (The color purple is the stranger because it is not a shape.) Increase the number of similar words you include in the group as soon as you think your child is ready for more than four. Be sure to allow him or her to give you a list of words which contain a "stranger." Talk about the reason a particular word does not belong.

## 35. Words Used for Comparison

Use words such as bigger, smaller; taller, shorter; higher, lower; thinner, fatter; round, rounder, roundest; wide, wider, widest; narrow, narrower, narrowest. Play comparison games by asking:

What is as fast as...?
As slow as...?
As soft as...?
As hard as...?
As sweet as...?
As sour as...?

## 36. Words About Positions In Space

Be specific when you use words such as: in and out, up and down, over and under, above and below, beneath, beside, between, and alongside, so that your child can understand the meaning of these abstract concepts.

## 37. The Adverbs Only Game

Use a variety of adverbs to give your child directions to be followed. (Adverbs are words that usually end in "ly.") *Walk quickly. Chew noisily. Sit quietly. Sing loudly. Talk happily. Skip gaily.*

# Environmental Awareness

*Help your child become an aware
observer of the world in which she or he lives.
Stress the words which describe that world.*

### 38. Shapes Around Us

Talk about and identify the varied
shapes of things that are found inside
and outside your home.  For example:
round pots, square TV set, rectangular
doors, windows of different shapes.

Go on a shape
identification hunt.
How many different
shapes can you find
and identify?

### 39. Colors Around Us

Talk about the colors of clothing, toys, cars, foods, signs, and houses. Refer to things by their color when you speak about them. For example: your red coat, the blue bus, the black and silver train.

### 40. Learn Color Poems
#### I. Traffic Lights

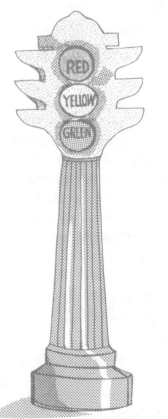

<u>Red, Yellow, Green</u>
Red is up
Green is down
And yellow is in the middle,
You know.

Red says, "Stop"
Green says, "Go"
And yellow says,
"Please go slow."

## II. Colors (crayons)

Magic Colors
I have some magic colors
So I can draw a scene
Of everything that's pretty
In yellow, red, or green
Or orange, blue, or purple
And some colors in between.

Maybe I'll draw a garden
There are lots of colors there
Roses, daisies, tulips
Growing everywhere.
And I won't forget those trees so
high
Reaching way, way up to the sky.

The following activities will provide many opportunities for vocabulary growth as well as extensive discussions of some basic science understandings.

## 41. Seasonal Changes

Go on a seasonal discovery walk or drive. Look for signs of seasonal changes, for example: temperatures, leaves changing colors, days becoming longer, flowers budding, snow on the ground. How will the changes affect your family? Your child? What holidays occur during various seasons?

## 42. Season Chart

Draw a large circle on a piece of tag board or cardboard. Divide the circle into four equal parts. Label each section with the name of a season (summer, fall, winter, spring). Paste pictures of clothing, holiday items, or recreational activities in the appropriate sections.

### 43. Animal Attributes

Play a guessing game by describing an animal and its habitat. For example:

*"I have two legs. I can live in many different kinds of homes. What kind of animal am I?"* (man, woman, person)

*"I have no fur. I can live in the water or on the ground. What kind of animal am I?"* (frog)

*"I have no eyes. I live under the ground. What kind of animal am I?"* (worm)

*"I have only two legs. I like to build nests for my family. What kind of animal am I?"* (bird)

Take turns making up the guessing question. (Refer to a picture book about animals if you are not sure of your information.)

### 44. Plant Care

Allow your child to take care of her or his own plants. Try to provide a variety of plants so that plants with different shaped and textured leaves can be observed. What do plants need in order to live?

### 45. Watch Things Grow

**I.** Place two or three toothpicks in a white or sweet potato. Suspend the potato in a jar or tumbler that is filled about two-thirds of the way with water. Watch as new growth takes place. (Be sure that at least two *eyes* are in the water.)

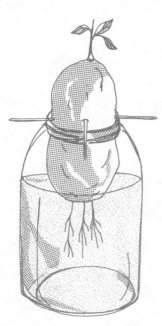

**II.** Cut the top off a carrot and place it in a saucer of water. Watch the new growth that takes place in a few days.

**III.** Plant an orange or grapefruit seed in some potting soil. Water it regularly. Record how long it takes to sprout, how many leaves it has, and how much it has grown in a month.

**IV.** Experiment with other seeds and beans that you use in your home. Compare different seeds and the way that they grow. Which took a long time to sprout? Which need more light? Which need more water? (Popcorn kernels grow quickly.)

Chapter

5

Activities to
Promote
Motor
Control and
Eye-Hand
Coordination

# *Activities to Promote Motor Control and Eye-Hand Coordination*

*Children need many opportunities to develop left and right body coordination, body balance, and eye-hand coordination.*

## 46. Rhythms

Listen and dance to music you both enjoy. Try different steps such as, skating, spinning, or marching in time to the music.

## 47. Follow the Leader

Take turns being follower and leader. Jump, clap, hop, bend, walk backwards, skip, slide, and glide.

## 48. Feed the Animals

Place one or more stuffed animals at one end of a room. Place a peanut, a grape, or a piece of an apple on a ruler. Child must carry the ruler across the room to the animal without dropping the object. If the child is successful, then he or she may eat the nut, grape, or apple.

*Variation:*

*When this task gets to be very easy for your child, make it more challenging by increasing the distance that the ruler must be carried, by adding more things to be carried, or by using other round objects, such as shelled or dried peas, beans, or small beads.*

## 49. Bead Stringing

Use pre-packaged wooden or plastic beads or make your own kits using shoelaces, large buttons, or any other objects which can be strung.

*Variations:*
  *I. String beads according to specific design or color pattern.*
  *II. Use assorted shapes of pasta for stringing. These can be painted either before or after they have been strung.*

**Note:** The painting and coating activities help develop motor coordination skills, too.

## 50. Sorting Activities

Add small blocks, screws of various sizes, nails, or bolts, to some of the beads and buttons used in the previous activity. Ask your child to group them by color, function, and/or shape.

**Note:** This is another good classification activity. It can also be used to talk about likenesses and differences.

## 51. Folding

Fold papers according to a design or pattern. You can make fans, hats, or airplanes. The fan is the easiest one to make. Fold a piece of paper back and forth lengthwise. Each fold should be about a half inch in width.

## 52. Hammering and Sawing

Supervised hammering and sawing of assorted blocks of soft, smooth wood are excellent activities for using both large and small muscles. Provide additional eye-hand coordination experience by encouraging your child to paint and decorate the finished product.

## 53. Cutting

Cut paper or fabric into random shapes, or follow a pattern or template. Cut pictures from magazines, newspapers, or catalogs.

### 54. Making Models

Use clay, play dough, plasticine, or other pliable materials to shape into free form objects or preformed molds. Encourage your child to use his or her imagination and to be as creative as possible. Talking about what she or he is doing is an important part of all these activities.

### 55. Pouring

Pour a liquid from one container to another. Pour soft solids such as sand, sugar, or flour from one container to another.

**Note:** This activity helps to develop an understanding of methods of measurement, and recognition of the relationship between shapes of containers and the quantities they can hold.

## 56. Puzzles

Colorful puzzles that fit into sturdy frames are excellent for developing a sense of spatial relationships and noting details.

**Note:** Color coding or numbering the backs of puzzle pieces makes it easier to keep track of where they belong.

## 57. Dress-Up

Keep a chest full of assorted "grown-up" clothes for role-playing. Playing dress-up and assuming different roles helps to develop motor coordination and promotes language usage and development.

## 58. Old Magazines

Keep a supply of old magazines and catalogs on hand. These can be used for refining cutting skills. Start a scrap book on a topic of interest by looking for, and cutting out, appropriate pictures. This will help to develop classification and eye-hand skills. For example, a scrapbook of trees, people, or cars.

## 59. Blocks

Blocks of various sizes and types provide many opportunities to develop both large and small muscle dexterity as well as eye-hand coordination. Blocks can be stacked straight up or placed side by side. Make a design with three or four blocks and have your child duplicate the pattern. Add more blocks when you think your child can comfortably handle a larger number of blocks.

## Chapter

# 6

**Listening
Skills**

*Good listening skills are an essential
part of reading development. Children must
be able to organize and interpret the
information they hear. They must have the
ability to recognize the difference between
sounds and words that are similar, and be
able to remember previously heard sound
stimuli.*

### 60. Travel Phonics

While traveling in a car, bus, or train,
or just walking, look for objects or signs
that start with the same sounds. For
example:
car, cane,
cage, or
baby,
booth,
book.

REST AREA

### 61. We Are Going To ...

Begin by saying, "We are going to Connecticut and we will buy cookies." The next person mentions something else "we will buy" beginning with the letter "C." When all possibilities have been exhausted choose another "letter" destination - preferably one that the child knows.

### 62. Rhyme Time

Start by saying a word that has an ending that can be rhymed with other words.

**Examples:** band, stand, hand, land, sand; cat, hat, sat; pig, wig, fig; ball, call, mall, stall.

Each person in turn must say a word that rhymes with the first word. When all rhymes for a specific word have been used, the last player to give a rhyming word chooses a new word for the game. You can make this a memory game by having each person repeat what has already been said.

### 63. I Spy

Start by saying, "I spy something with my little eye that starts with the letter..." You have to have seen the object. Your child must guess what you "spy" and then gets a turn to "spy" something else by telling you what letter it begins with. You must guess what she or he "spies."

### 64. Stranger in the Rhyming Family

Pronounce a series of rhyming words such as glad, bad, had, mad. Include a non-rhyming word such as book. Child must identify the "stranger" and then say why the word doesn't belong with the others.

### 65. Muffin Man

Sing or say the nursery rhyme:

"Oh, do you know the muffin man,
　the muffin man, the muffin man
Oh, do you know the muffin man
　who lives on Drury Lane?"
"Oh, yes I know the muffin man,
　the muffin man, the muffin man
Oh, yes I know the muffin man.  His
　name begins with ...M"

*Variations:*

*I. Change the name of the lane to one which starts with the letter "M."*

*II. Change the occupation to baker man, candy man, fireman... Each time you change the occupation change the name of the lane so that they both start with the same sound. The last line must say what the name begins with.*

### 66. Follow My Sound

Demonstrate two or three different sounds in succession. For example: clap twice, tap on a table three times, stamp your foot. Your actions must be repeated in the same order and number as you did them. Start very simply and then add more actions as your child becomes successful at this task.

### 67. What Kind of Animal Are You?

Allow each person in a group to choose an animal that she or he would like to be. Decide on a sound that will represent each animal. Tell a story which names each of the animals chosen. Your child must make the sound of the animal every time it is mentioned in the story.

### 68. What's Wrong with Mother Goose?

After your child is thoroughly familiar with several of the traditional nursery rhymes, change one or two of the ending words. See if she/he can discover the incorrect word(s) and then tell you what the correct one(s) should be.

### 69. Going On a Picnic

Start by saying, "We're going on a picnic and we will take hot dogs." The next player must repeat the sentence and add another item to take. Each player must repeat all the previously mentioned items before adding another item.

### 70. Music

Listen to music tapes or records together. Try to differentiate the sounds that each instrument makes. Talk about the difference between loud and soft music, fast and slow music, happy and sad music.

### 71. Homemade Musical Instruments

Empty juice cans, paper plates laced or stapled together and filled with dried beans or pebbles, water glasses and jars filled with different amounts of liquids, all make musical sounds which you and your child can listen to, talk about, and enjoy together.

### 71. Guess What I Am

Decide on a category such as sounds in the kitchen, sounds on the playground, sounds in a store. Player must make a sound that might be heard in the designated category. The other players must guess what it is. The person who guesses correctly can then make another sound to be guessed.

### 73. What Sounds Do You Hear?

Make or obtain a tape of such sounds as a plane flying overhead, a clock ticking, a motorcycle roaring, a siren blowing, a fire truck, a train... Have your child listen to the tape and try to identify the sounds.

### 74. Rhyming Riddles

Make up simple riddles which your child must complete with a rhyming word.

**Examples:**
I like to skip and run
When I play in the _____. *(sun)*

When I was three
I couldn't climb a _____. *(tree)*

My mom can bake
a chocolate _____. *(cake)*

### 75. Listen and Draw

Read a poem or story that has very descriptive and colorful words. When you have finished reading, ask your child to draw pictures of what she/he has just heard. See how many details are included in the pictures.

# Following Oral Directions

*The ability to listen to and then follow a series of oral directions is a necessary skill children should learn. You can prepare your child for this activity by making a game of it in an informal, stress-free manner. As in all other activities, start with very simple tasks. Make them more complex as your child is able to follow them successfully.*

## 76. One Step Directions

"Fold your hands." "Go to the door." "Put the book back on the shelf."

## 77. Two Step Directions

"Sit on the floor, then touch you nose." "Hop two times, then close your eyes."

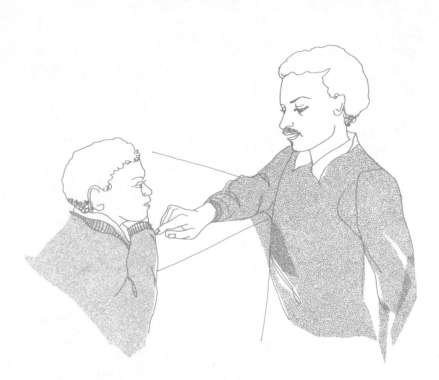

### 78. Three Step Directions

"Pick up the ball, put it in the basket, then clap your hands." "Open the door, look outside, then come sit in my lap."

### 79. Four Step Directions

"Turn around, sit down, close your eyes, and tap your foot one time."

### 80. Silly Sentences

Tell your child to listen carefully as you say some *silly sentences*. Your child should be able to tell you why they are silly and then restate them correctly.

**Examples:** Ice cream tastes very hot. Peaches and watermelon swim in the ocean. Only babies can drive cars. Onions and garlic are good desserts.

### 81. Simon Says

Tell your children that they may follow the command only if "Simon says" is heard before the command is given.

**Example:**
Leader says,
"Simon says clap hands.
Simon says hands on hips.
Touch your toes."
*(The child shouldn't do this last command because Simon didn't say.)*

# Sensory Awareness

*Literacy begins with the impressions we get through our senses. It is important to make your child aware of the messages that come from her/his senses, especially the visual (seeing), the auditory (hearing), and the tactile (touching).*

### 82. Use Your Senses

Make your child aware of her/his senses by talking about things that you can touch, taste, see, hear, and smell. Go for a walk and touch different kinds of leaves. Smell the aromas in a bakery. Hear a lawn mower or the sounds of different vehicles. See a garden. Look in a store window.

*Variations:*

*Talk about good sounds/bad sounds; things that feel nice to touch/things that don't feel nice; good smells/bad smells; pleasant things to see/unpleasant things to see.*

## 83. Make a "Feelie" Box

Collect scraps of fabric, paper, wood, or metal of different sizes. Put them in a box. Child closes eyes, reaches into box, feels an object, and tries to guess what it is.

**Note:** Encourage your child to talk about how the object feels--its texture, its shape, its size, while trying to guess what it is.

*Variations:*

*I. Child must use a specific number of words as she/he describes the object. Listener or other player must guess what it is from the description.*

*II. Place different shaped items such as nuts, square blocks, pencils, keys, in the box. Child must describe the shape and guess the item.*

**Note:** Be sure to change the contents of the box from time to time.

# Body Awareness

*Children need to have an awareness of their bodies and the relationships of their body parts to themselves and their environment.*

### 84. Body Parts Song

(Sung to the tune of "Frere Jacques")
Child must point to each body part as it is sung.

**Where Is My Nose?**

Where is my nose?
Where is your nose?
Here's my nose.
See my nose.
Pozey, Rozey, Nozey!
Pozey, Rozey, Nozey!
See my nose.
See my nose.

### Where is My Hand?

Where is my hand?
Where is your hand?
Here's my hand.
See my hand.
Sandy, Candy, Handy!
Sandy, Candy, Handy!
See my hand.
See my hand.

### Where is My Tooth?

Where is my tooth?
Where is your tooth?
Here's my tooth.
See my tooth.
Poothy, moothy, toothy!
Poothy, moothy, toothy!
See my tooth.
See my tooth.

**Note:** Make up similar verses for other body parts.

## 85. Learn Finger Plays

(Finger plays are short poems which use hand movements to illustrate the action.)

### I. Going to School

One little house shut up tight...
*(Right fist is clenched.)*
Open the door and there in sight...
*(Open fist and spread fingers.)*
Are one..two..three..four..five little children, tall and straight...
*(Raise a finger for each count.)*
Ready for pre-school. Now don't be late.
*(Fingers "run" into cupped left hand.)*

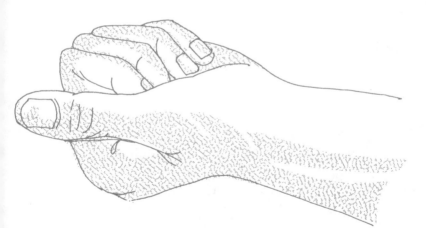

## II. Where Is Thumbkin?
(To the tune of "Frere Jacques" )

*(Child holds closed hand behind her/his
back while singing.)*
Where is thumbkin?
Where is thumbkin?
Here I am!
Here I am!
*(Bring hand to front. Hold up thumb.)*
How are you this morning?
Very well, I thank you.
*(Flex thumb up and down.)*
Run away. Run away.
*(Hand goes behind back again.)*

Repeat the verse calling out
different fingers in sequence:  pointer,
tall person, ring person,and pinkie.
When all fingers have been called out,
change the last line to:

Stay and play.
Stay and play.
*(Clap both hands.)*

## 86. Dance and Perform the Actions to Songs

Play songs like "Looby Loo" or "Hokey Pokey."

In addition to increasing body awareness, both of these dances emphasize direction discrimination.

**I. Looby Loo**
Here we go looby loo,
Here we go looby light,
Here we go looby loo,
All on a Saturday night,

Here we go to the left,
Here we go to the right,
Here we go to the left,
All on a Saturday night,

Make up your own verses.

Repeat Looby Loo verse each time you do the actions for a different direction: Up/down, back/front, near/far.

## II. Hokey Pokey

For this circle dance, certain body parts are put into the circle and then they are taken out of the circle.

You put your left hand in,
You take your left hand out,
You put your left hand in,
And you shake it all about,
You do the Hokey Pokey,
And you turn yourself around,
That's what it's all about.

Repeat with these body parts:
right hand
left leg
right leg
left elbow
right elbow...
End with whole self.

# Auditory and Visual Discrimination Activities

*Reading involves the ability to discriminate among letters, shapes, and words that are similar in appearance. It also requires the ability to discriminate between different, though similar, sounds.*

### 87. Match the Picture to the Sound

**Materials:**
9x12 tag board or cardboard
a large envelope
pictures cut from magazines, old books, and newspapers

**Directions:**
Paste a stimulus picture on the top left side of the cardboard and another picture on the top right side.

*Example:*

A boat and a lamp. Cut out small pictures of objects that start with the sounds of each of the stimulus pictures. Place the pictures in the envelope and paste the envelope to the back of the card.

*Activity:*

Child takes pictures from the envelope and places them under the appropriate stimulus picture. Be sure to have child talk about why the pictures are placed on a particular.

Make a separate card for each pair of sounds with which you are working. Add to or change the pictures as your child becomes more competent at this task.

## 88. Left/Right Discrimination

Lay out several pictures or objects in a row. Each one must be identified in order from left to right.

## 89. What's Missing?

Place several objects on a table. Allow child to study them for one minute then close her/his eyes while you remove one of the objects. Child must be able to tell you what is missing. This activity will help to develop visual memory.

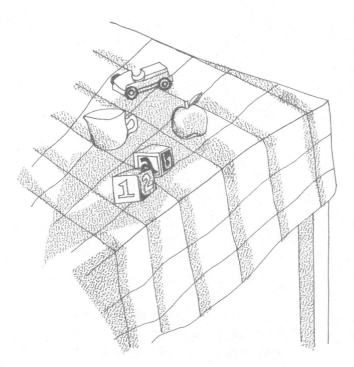

*Variations:*

*I. If you have a slate or chalkboard, write several alphabet letters or numbers randomly on board. Child closes eyes while you erase a letter (or number). Child must then tell you tell you what is missing.*

*II. Use magnetic letters or numbers. Place them on a metal surface such as a refrigerator. Follow the same procedure as above.*

**Note:** Be sure your child is thoroughly familiar with the letters and numbers you use for this activity.

### 90. Same or Different?

Pronounce pairs of words that start with the same sound (big-bag, can-cake, rat-rope). Child must tell you when the words start with the same sound and when they start with a different sound. If your child can, ask her/him to tell you the sounds the words start with.

*Variation:*

Pronounce a series of three or more words starting with the same sound. Include a word that starts with a different sound. Child must say which words start the same, which one is different.

# Storytelling Activities

*Children are natural story tellers and should be encouraged to develop this ability. Storytelling requires the teller to organize her/his thoughts into units that have a beginning, a middle, and an end. Telling stories prepares children for writing stories, too.*

*Children love to listen to stories, especially stories about family members and events. Listening to stories provides another opportunity for developing good auditory skills.*

## 91. Favorite Heirloom

Tell about a favorite family heirloom. Stories about how it was acquired, how old it is, and who owned it last, give children a valuable sense of family belonging.

## 92. Favorite Stories

Tell stories about a favorite relative, a special event, a trip, a favorite teacher, a funny adventure. Use as many descriptive words as you can to make the story more interesting.

## 93. "Round Robin" Stories

One person starts to tell a story and stops at a crucial point. The next person continues the story and stops at another point. Continue in this manner until everyone agrees that the story is complete.

*Variations:*

*I. Tape record the story so your child can listen to it at any time.*

*II. Write or type the story and add it to your family library. Allow your child to illustrate it.*

*III. Start another story with the same beginning. All other characters and places must be changed.*

*IV. Start a new story which must have the same ending as the original story.*

## 94. "Just Imagine" Stories

Start by saying:
"Just imagine if flower petals became gumdrops when they fell off."
**or**
"Just imagine if it really rained cats and dogs."
**or**
"Just imagine if animal crackers could talk."

Ask your child to tell what would happen or to think of other situations that are equally as silly.

Suggest to your child that she/he pretend to be a leaf, a pencil, a book...

Ask: "What do you look like?"
"How do you feel?"
"What are some things that have happened to you?"

Encourage your child to be as creative as possible with her/his responses.

# Writing Activities

*Provide your child with pencils, crayons, felt tip pens, and a variety of paper. This will allow her/him to experiment with and explore writing as a means of communication. Take the time to write down ideas or messages that your child dictates. By doing this you are showing her/him that talk can be recorded and read at another time. This is another way of emphasizing the value of reading.*

### 96. "All About Me" Book
Buy a notebook or make a blank book by stapling or sewing pages together. Paste pictures of your child in the book. Write captions that your child dictates to you under each picture. Label some of the blank pages with such captions as: *Me, When I'm Happy. Me, When I'm Sad. My Family. My Favorite Food.* Ask your child to draw appropriate pictures for each heading.

## 97. Art Stories

When your child has drawn a picture, ask what, if anything, you should write about it. Remember that these are your child's ideas so don't try to change them. Remember to title the picture story.

My house.

## 98. Happy Happenings Book

Label a blank notebook with your child's name and the title "Happy Happenings." Each day have him/her tell you one or two sentences about a "happy happening." Record the date on each page and encourage your child to illustrate the sentences. She or he could also draw pictures of what she or he looked like during the "happy happening."

## 99. Write a Book Together

Ask your child to examine a toy or any object closely and then tell you exactly what it looks like. Include descriptions of the size, shape, color, and texture. Write each sentence on a separate piece of paper. Number the pages in the order that the sentences were told to you. Ask your child to illustrate each page. Decide on a title for the book and print it in large letters on a separate cover page. Be sure to print your child's name under the title and explain that she or he is the author of the book.

*Variations:*

*I. Write a story about an event or an idea instead of a toy or object.*

*For example: My Best Birthday, When I Lost My Tooth, Going To The Circus, Playing In The Snow.*

*II. Write a "Make-believe" story together. Talk about the characters who will be in the story, what they look like, where they live, and what kinds of things happened to them. Then write the story as your child dictates it.*

### 100. Weather Stories

Talk about and draw pictures of: what rain looks like, what rain sounds like, what snow looks like, what snow sounds like, what you can do on a summer day, and what you can do on a winter day. Write captions under each picture.

We can build a snowman.

### 101. Stories from Pictures

Cut pictures from magazines, catalogs, newspapers, and old books. Talk about the pictures.

What kind of stories do they tell? What is special about them? What do you think will happen to the people in the picture? Write down your child's reactions and responses to the picture. Encourage her/him to tell a story that has a beginning, middle, and end.

# *Afterword*

The activities described in this book should be fun for you and your child. They can and should be modified to suit your needs. They are not intended to be formal lessons, nor should they be used as such.

Above all, these activities should enable you and your child to expand and enrich the ways in which you communicate. Providing your child with a broad range of positive language experiences should prepare her/him for successful literacy learning mastery in school.

We have listed 101 books which can be found in your public library. They will provide you and your child with a starting point **On The Road To Reading.**

## *Have fun!*

Allen, Pamela
*Fancy That!*
Orchard Books, 1988

Anno, Mitsumasa
*Anno's Peekaboo*
Philomel Books, 1987

Asch, Frank
*Oak and Wild Apples*
Holiday House, 1988

Bang, Molly G.
*Ten, Nine, Eight*
Greenwillow, 1983

Bemmelmans, Ludwig
*Madeline*
Viking, 1939

Bohdal, Susi
*Bobby the Bear*
North-South Books, 1986

Bohdal, Susi
*Harry the Hare*
North-South Books, 1986

Bond, Michael
*Paddington at the Zoo*
G. P. Putman's Sons, 1985

Brown, Marc
*Hand Rhymes*
E. P. Dutton, 1985

Brown, Marc, compiler
*Play Rhymes*
E. P. Dutton, 1987

Burton, Virginia L.
*The Little House*
Houghton, 1942

Caple, Kathy
*The Purse*
Houghton Mifflin, 1986

Carle, Eric
*The Very Busy Spider*
Putnam, 1981

Carlstrom, Nancy White
*The Moon Came Too*
Macmillan, 1987

Cleary, Beverly
*Janet's Thingamajigs*
Dell/Young Yearling Special Books, 1987

Clifton, Lucille
*Everett Anderson's Nine Month Long*
Holt, 1978

Cohen, Miriam
*Starring First Grade*
Greenwillow, 1985

Cooney, Barbara
*Miss Rumphius*
Viking, 1982

Dale, Penny
*Bet You Can't*
J. P. Lippincott, 1987

Davidson, Amanda
*Teddy in the Garden*
Holt, Rinehart and Winston, 1986

Gag, Wanda
*The A B C Bunny*
Coward, 1933

Gag, Wanda
*Millions of Cats*
Coward, 1928

Galdone, Paul
*Three Little Kittens*
Clarion Books, 1986

Gay, Michel
*Little Shoe*
Macmillan, 1986

Gay, Michel
*Take Me for a Ride*
Viking Penguin/Puffin Books, 1987

Gillham, Bill
*And So Can I!*
G. P. Putnam's Sons, 1987

Hall, Derek
*Polar Bear Leaps*
Alfred A. Knopf/Sierra Club, 1985

Harper, Anita
*Just a Minute!*
G. P. Putnam's Sons, 1987

Hill, Eric
*Spot's First Easter*
Putnam's Sons/Ventura Books,1988

Hines, Anna Grossnickle
*All by Myself*
Clarion Books, 1985

Hines, Anna Grossnickle
*It's Just Me, Emily*
Clarion Books, 1987

Hoban, Tana
*1, 2, 3*
Greenwillow Books, 1985

Hoban, Tana
*What Is It?*
Greenwillow Books, 1985

Hutchins, Pat
*Rosie's Walk*
Macmillan, 1968

Keats, Ezra J.
*Snowy Day*
Viking, 1962

Kightley, Rosalinda
*The Farmer*
Macmillan, 1987

Kightley, Rosalinda
*The Postman*
Macmillan, 1987

Kilroy, Sally
*Grandpa's Garden*
Viking Kestrel, 1986

Kilroy, Sally
*Market Day*
Viking Kestrel, 1986

Kilroy, Sally
*On the Road*
Viking Kestrel, 1986

Kilroy, Sally
*What a Week!*
Viking Kestrel, 1986

Kitamura, Satoshi
*Lily Takes a Walk*
E. P. Dutton, 1987

Kline, Suzy
*Don't Touch!*
Albert Whitman, 1985

Krauss, Ruth
*The Carrot Seed*
Harper and Row, 1945

Lloyd, David
*Duck*
J. B. Lippincot, 1988

Lynn, Sara
*Clothes*
Macmillan/Aladdin Books, 1986

Lynn, Sara
*Food*
Macmillan/Aladdin Books, 1986

Lynn, Sara
*Home*
Macmillan/Aladdin Books, 1986

Lynn, Sara
*Toys*
Macmillan/Aladdin Books, 1986

Manning, Paul
*Clown*
Macmillan/Merry-Go-Rhymes
Very First Books, 1988

Marahashi, Keiko
*I Have a Friend*
Margaret K. McElderry Books, 1987

McCloskey, Robert
*Blueberries for Sal*
Viking, 1948

McPhail, David
*The Dream Child*
E.P. Dutton/Unicorn Books, 1985

Morgan, Michaela
*Visitors for Edward*
E. P. Dutton, 1987

Mueller, Virginia
*Monster and the Baby*
Albert Whitman, 1985

Pfister, Marcus
*Where Is My Friend?*
North-South Books, 1986

Politi, Leo
*The Nicest Gift*
Scribner, 1973

Pooley, Sarah, compiler
*A Day of Rhymes*
Alfred A. Knopf/Borzoi Books, 1987

Riddell. Chris
*Ben and the Bear*
J. B. Lippincott, 1986

Roffey, Maureen
*Family Scramble*
E. P. Dutton, 1987

Roffey, Maureen
*Fantasy Scramble*
E. P. Dutton, 1987

Roffey, Maureen
*I Spy at the Zoo*
four Winds Press/I Spy Books, 1988

Roffey, Maureen
*I Spy on Vacation*
Four Winds Press/I Spy Books, 1988

Roffey, Maureen
*Look, There's My Hat!*
G. P. Putnam's Sons, 1985

Schmid, Eleonore
*Farm Animals*
North-South Books, 1986

Scott, Ann Herbert
*Sam*
McGraw-Hill, 1967

Shannon, George
*Oh, I Love!*
Bradbury Press, 1988

Sheldon, Dyan
*I Forgot*
Four Winds Press, 1988

Slobodkina, Esphyr
*Caps for Sale*
Harper Junior Books, 1947

Stoddard, Sandol
*Bedtime for Bear*
Houghton Mifflin, 1985

Sutherland, Harry
*Dad's Car Wash*
Atheneum, 1988

Taylor, Jud
*My Cat*
Macmillan, 1988

Taylor, Judy
*My Dog*
Macmillan, 1988

Turkle, Brinton
*Deep in the Forest*
Dutton, 1976

Wahl, Jan
*Humphrey's Bear*
Henry Holt, 1987

Ward, Cindy
*Cookies's Week*
C. P. Putnam's Sons, 1988

Ward, Lund
*The Biggest Bear*
Houghton, 1972

Weiss, Nicki
*Barney Is Big*
Greenwilow Books, 1988

Wells, Rosemary
*Max's Bath*
Dial Books for Young Readers
                Very First Books, 1985

Wells, Rosemary
*Max's Bedtime*
Dial Books for Young Readers
Very First Books, 1985

Wells, Rosemary
*Max's Birthday*
Dial Books for Young Readers
Very First Books, 1985

Wells, Rosemary
*Max's Breakfast*
Dial Books for Young Readers
Very First Books, 1985

Wells, Rosemary
*Forest of Dreams*
Dial Books for Young Readers, 1988

Wells, Rosemary
*Max's Christmas*
Dial Books for Young Readers, 1986

Winter, Jeanette
*Come Out to Play*
Alfred A. Knopf/Borzoi Books, 1986

Winthrop, E.
*Shoes*
Harper and Row, 1986

Yektai, Niki
*What's Missing?*
Clarion Books, 1987

Zemach, Margot
*Hush, Little Baby*
E. P. Dutton/Unicorn Books, 1987

Ziefert, Harriet
*Lewis Said, Lewis Did!*
Random House, 1987

Ziefert, Harriet
*Nicky's Friend*
Viking Kestrel, 1986

Ziefert, Harriet
*Nicky's Noisy Night*
Viking Kestrel, 1986

Ziefert, Harriet
*No, No, Nicky*
Viking Kestrel, 1986

Ziefert, Harriet
*Where's the Cat?*
Harper and Row, 1987

Ziefert, Harriet
*Where's the Dog?*
Harper and Row, 1987

Ziefert, Harriet
*Where's the Turtle?*
Harper and Row, 1987

Zinnemann-Hope, Pam
*Let's Play Ball, Ned*
Margaret K. McElderry Books, 1986

Zinnemann-Hope, Pam
*Time for Bed, Ned*
Margaret K. McElderry Books, 1986

Zion, Gene
*Harry the Dirty Dog*
Harper Junior Books, 1956

Zolotow, Charlotte
*William's Doll*
Harper Junior Books, 1972

Zolotow, Charlotte
*Sleepy Book*
Harper and Row, 1986

# About the Author

***Beatrice G. Davis, M.S., P. D.*** has been a reading educator, education writer, consultant, and author for more than thirty years. She has conducted special training programs for parents, teachers, para-professionals, administrators, and students at regional, state, and local reading conferences. She has been a guest speaker and a parent workshop leader on numerous occasions. Ms. Davis has chaired reading conferences at the local level and has served on planning committees for state and national conferences. She has had several articles printed in general interest magazines. Ms. Davis has taught at every level from nursery school through college.

# About the Illustrator

*Sheila Wigglesworth* grew up in New York City and is a product of the New York City Public School system. She has received a Bachelors of Fine Arts degree in Art Education from the University of the Arts in Philadelphia, Pennsylvania. She also holds a Masters of Fine Arts in Painting from Pratt Institute in Brooklyn, New York.

Ms. Wigglesworth has taught Art in the New York City Public School system for over 15 years. She has exhibited at galleries in New York, Pennsylvania, and Connecticut. Her work is owned by private collectors throughout the United States.